SPIRIT OF TIME AND PLACE

Prayer-thoughts, Praise-poems and Words of Worship

by Cliff Reed

with illustrations by Lyanne Mitchell

The Lindsey Press
London
2002

Published by the Lindsey Press
on behalf of the General Assembly of Unitarian and Free
Christian Churches, Essex Hall, 1-6 Essex Street, London WC2R
3HY

ISBN 0 85319 068 2

Printed by FM Repro Ltd.
69 Lumb Lane, Roberttown, Liversedge, West Yorkshire WF15 7NB
Telephone: 01924 411011 Fax: 01924 411196
Email: fmrepro@aol.com

CONTENTS

INTRODUCTION

I started today with a walk on the beach. The sun cast a golden causeway across the uncharacteristically blue North Sea. Some sea-anglers were hunched on the surf-washed shingle. Morning light bathed this quiet little town. A few walkers took the air. I stood on the sea-smoothed pebbles and quietly said my morning prayer.

Such moments come to me in many places - and not only ones as peaceful and beautiful as this! Sometimes they bring pain and disquiet rather than tranquility and exaltation. And there is something about the specificity of time and place that moves me - that it was on this day in this place that I had this experience.

The circling earth, the cycles of nature, the festivals and commemorations we have made - all speak (if we will listen) of the Divine Unity, the dynamic power of God with which we are alive. Whether alone on a beach, or in a city street, or together in our meeting-houses and churches, it is by allowing ourselves to feel divinity within and around us that we know the presence - here, now - of eternal life.

The contents of this book speak of times and places when I felt something I can only call divine, and of my attempts to help others do the same.

Cliff Reed
Aldeburgh, Suffolk
November

SPIRIT OF TIME AND PLACE

Spirit of this time and this place
open my soul to wonder
and my heart to love -
now, here.

Spirit of Time and Place

Saelig Suffolk

Saelig - later degraded to 'silly' - means 'blessed' or 'holy' in Anglo-Saxon. It was applied to Suffolk from a very early date, referring to the exceptionally high number of churches and monastic foundations in the county in Anglo-Saxon times. It owes much to the great shrine of East Anglia's martyr-king, Saint Edmund, which was situated in Suffolk from the ninth to the sixteenth centuries, until destroyed by Henry VIII. The Suffolk landscape is still a sacred one, and not just because of its over five hundred medieval churches - some on earlier Christian and Pagan sites. It also has some fine examples of seventeenth and eighteenth century dissenting meeting houses, three of them now Unitarian.

A WINTER'S DAY

Fynn Valley, Suffolk, 7th December 1998

The sort of day that no-one writes about.
Dull and wet, insidiously cold;
but a heron rises from the meadow,
majestic on soft grey wings.
Redwings dart across the fields
where winter wheat breaks green
through dark earth.

Yes, there is beauty here.
How glad I am that I ventured out.

BREATH OF GOD

Fynn Valley, Suffolk, 12th June 2000

Summer breeze is playing over grass.
I breathe it in, the breath of life,
As Adam breathed it once in Eden
from the mouth of God.

SWALLOW
Alton Water, Suffolk, 14th June 1999

Suddenly -
an iridescent deep-blue sheen
sweeping low over nodding grass:
a swallow passes by.

AFTER OMAGH: 15th AUGUST 1998
In the Fynn Valley

So much beauty in a summer sky -
  may its glory touch the dead hearts of those who hate
  and make them live.

SUMMER'S END
North Warren, Suffolk, 6th September 1999

On a warm September afternoon
  butterflies suck sweetness
  from succulent blackberries -
  Comma, Red Admiral and Speckled Wood
  resplendent in the sun.

The year is at its fatness
  and soon must fade,
  but for now the butterflies and I
  cling on to summer.

RAINBOW'S END
Fynn Valley, Suffolk, 26th October 1998

I turned, and there it was!
- within this sparkling golden valley,
- behind the naked poplars' fanlike filigree.
Yes, there it was - the rainbow's end!
A moment to give thanks before I think.
So, thank you!

ARMISTICE DAY IN THE PARK
Christchurch Park, Ipswich, 11th November 2000

Up they rise in frantic charge
- beautiful in uniforms of russet-brown -
across the grass, over their rotting comrades
at the senseless wind's command.
And then they fall.

THE SPARROWHAWK
Thorpeness, Suffolk, 23rd November 1998

Straight he flew
- utterly focused, intent on prey -
below the raised beach on which I sat,
watching a millpond sea.
He passed beneath my feet,
oblivious of my presence,
went on unswervingly.

O that I might have such clarity.

SEA AND SKY

Shingle Street, Suffolk, 28th February 1998

Pied piping oystercatchers pass overhead
where, wispy-white, clouds stream across the blue.
On the glittering sea, ships out of Felixstowe
punctuate the horizon.
Gulls gather on shingle banks
and cormorants hang themselves out to dry.
In the midst of sea and sky I glimpse eternity.

ON THE BEACH

Near Thorpeness, July 1997

When we are gone,
with all our passion, pride and questing thought,
the sea will still lap upon the shore.

MOMENTS LIKE THESE

Ipswich, 1st March 2000

Sitting back from my reading and sipping my coffee,
I look out the window to where the birds are feeding.
A collared-dove, a blackbird, a few house-sparrows
- nothing very exotic! -
and yet it's moments like these that charm the day
and keep me going.

BY THE RIVER DEBEN BELOW WOODBRIDGE
25th January 1999

The Anglo-Saxon royal burial site at Sutton Hoo stands above the Deben outside Woodbridge. The famous ship-burial, excavated there in 1939, is believed to be that of Raedwald, seventh century king of East Anglia. It contained a priceless collection of artefacts.

Mudflats glisten in the winter sun,
shining as it always has and always will.
On this gentle river Norsemen sailed,
bringing trade or terror to the little town -
still clustered round its house of God.

Sheldduck gleam and curlew cry -
as they did a thousand years ago and more
when ancient kings were laid to rest
upon the farther shore.

THE MASK OF SUMMER SLIPS
Fynn Valley, Suffolk, 14th September 1998

The mask of summer slips.
The trees are green, but tell-tale leaves are letting go.
Bracken too is not yet brown, but it has a beaten look.
A kestrel wheels across bare harvest fields,
where the ploughman is already at his lonely work.
A wind is sighing in the woods that is no summer breeze.
Beneath the clouds it brings a chill that wasn't there a week ago.
Martins and swallows still swoop and chatter, but leaving is on their minds. A hornet wanders aimless and weary at my feet.
Autumn gathers her strength.
Spirit of the Earth, strengthen us to face the fall,
and learn her lessons.

THE CHURCH OF THE OPEN SKY

Fynn Valley, Suffolk, 18th May 1998

This is a place where I worship
on a day that I keep holy.

Carpeted and furnished in a myriad shades of living green;
the ceiling - infinite blue.
Heat and light are free, pouring abundant life into fabric and
worshippers alike.

The choir sings with many voices, many songs,
but all seems harmony to me:
the rhythmic chiffchaff, the whitethroat's scratchysweetness;
the black cap's brief pure melody, pheasant's raucous counterpoint
gentle purring of the turtle dove, ominous bass of crow;
explosive ecstasy of nightingale, the joyous mocking laughter of
the yaffle.

All these and more raise their chorus to the open sky,
where a skylark hymns the Gloria
and a soaring sparrowhawk silently proclaims the Dies Irae.

Below, irreverent rabbits scamper.
Bright beetles unwittingly fulfil their sacred purpose.
The Little Sisters of Industry toil unceasingly in selfless service of
their Goddess and their Queen.

Around me, waving grass bows as if in prayer
and butterflies dance their rites in vestments
more glorious than those of any priest.

Here, in this unbounded church I worship,
not alone but with all creation..
upon the farther shore.

FIELDFARES

Fynn Valley, 22nd February 1999

The fieldfare is a species of thrush that breeds in Scandinavia and northern Germany and winters in the British Isles. Suffolk saying: 'February-fill-the-dyke, black or white.' Freya is the Norse goddess of fertility and love.

A
field
full of
fieldfares on a bright
February day.
Fill-dyke flickers into spring, so a
fond
farewell I offer to these
frost-weather
friends -
flying soon to
forest margins
far away, the
fiefdoms of
Freya divine,
fertile and
fair.

MINSMERE IN DECEMBER
9th December 1997

Purple-headed reeds - dry and rattling in
the December wind.

Lead-hued, living sea, rolling in on shifting
shingle beneath a cold sky of blue and white
and shades of grey.

Steely, breeze-fanned waters of the mere:
bobbing brilliant upon them, shelduck, teal
and mallard - plumaged, almost, for spring.

Sunset bathes the russet bracken, the
grey-green trunks of forest oaks.

The year dies in beauty and in hope.

Give thanks!

WILDWOOD
Staverton Thicks, 18th October 1999

This is how it was - and how it should be -
in our sad denuded land.
The autumn sun emblazons gnarled contorted oaks,
millennium-old.
Dead birches lie where they fell
- untidied, fungus-fringed -
among these mighty holly trees.
This is the wildwood's sacred remnant,
where life still moves to ancient rhythms,
re-mothering the orphaned human soul.

Holy Lands, Holy Places

PRAYER AT IKEN CHURCH
29th November 1999

O God,
on this wet, grey
Advent Monday
I make this pilgrimage
once more.

Thank you for the beauty of this place,
and for its bird-haunted peace.
Thank you for this ancient church.

Fourteen-hundred years of prayer
have seeped into the ground
on which it stands,
fused with the stone
of tower, nave and chancel.

But they have not made it holy,
for holy it already was
when Saxon saints
first knew your presence here
and offered praise,
as I do now.
Amen.

AT BECKET'S SHRINE

Canterbury Cathedral, 14th December 2000

A sacred spot.
But why?
Because holy, blissful Thomas was murdered here?
Or because so many motley pilgrims -
from Chaucer's twenty-nine to me -
have stood and wondered how to feel,
with heads bowed

THE FLOWERY CROWN

Shaharout, Israel, 23rd March 1996

In the Wilderness there grows a thorn.

Its barbs are long and sharp,
designed to pierce and tear the flesh.

Its flowers are pink -
tiny, delicate, beautiful.

It blooms in spring, at Passover,
when its spines are fresh and green.

Was this the thorn from which the crown was made?
A flowery crown, bright with earth's new life?

Did blood flow through the beauty?

Did even this instrument of mockery and pain
witness to life's resurrection?

Witness to something deeper
than the tormentors ever knew?

JESUS AT TABGHA
Galilee, 25th March 1996

The pilgrim-tourists crowd the church at Tabgha:
spending their shekels in the gift shop,
listening to off-pat guides -
the shepherds of these faithful flocks
come in search of Jesus.

He fed five thousand here, they're told,
here on the Galilean lakeshore. Maybe he did,
but where is Jesus now in this new multitude?
Somehow, I don't see him where the tills jingle,
or even where the story is retold of ancient miracle.

Out where the buses stand there is a scruffy little cafe, filled
with smoke and lively conversation of the everyday. Here are
the bus drivers. People of this land. Here too, sipping coffee,
laughing with the rest, is Jesus - unnoticed by those
who came to find him.

MEDITATION ON MATTHEW 21:1-17, FOR PALM SUNDAY
Jerusalem, 31st March 1996

This seemed a day of hope, the day that Jesus rode into Jerusalem, gentle and mounted on a donkey: down the Mount of Olives, a steep and narrow road through groves and gardens.

Ahead: the city. High walls golden in the morning sun. Gates flung open for Passover pilgrims. Across the valley, mighty and magnificent, the Temple - with roofs and pinnacles agleam.

Down the Mount he rode: cavalcade growing, followers shouting, palm-branches waving.
From the city, from walls and rooftops they saw him.
Who was he? Was this their promised king?

'This is the prophet Jesus,' they are told, 'from Nazareth in Galilee.' Riding in to stake his claim. The narrow streets erupt in anger, joy and fear.

The Temple is cleansed, the sick are healed.
Jesus is acclaimed by children. The priests complain and are rebuked. Then he is gone - for now.

It was a day of hope, of foolish, fervid hope - but not, perhaps, for him. Jesus made his challenge and knew what it must mean.

Liberty is not so easily won - for body or for soul.
Let us be wary of easy salvation and those who offer it.
Gethsemane awaits, and Calvary.

FOR THE PEACE OF JERUSALEM
Psalm 122: 6,7; Luke 19: 42

We pray for the peace of Jerusalem.
May there be peace within her boundaries
and may all her people prosper.
We pray for the peace of the whole earth.
May all who share her know, this day,
thc way that leads to peace.

PENNSYLVANIA AUGUST
Cumberland County, 1998

Hummingbirds are on the mimosa;
Cicadas give voice to the lazy heat;
Shimmering blue-winged wasps cloud the catmint
and morning glory blooms purple in the yard.

A cardinal, red eminence on arching branch, presides
above the urban creek, where trout run in the spring.
Catbirds cry in the underbrush. Above the trail - improbably
perched - a woodchuck sleeps.
Great egrets grace this wetland fragment, and chickadees
this forest memory.

An indigo bunting - deep blue beauty in a sunset wood;
Turkey-vultures - skyborne optimists - ever present, ever
watchful, effortlessly wheeling.

The people?

Some dodging from one air-conditioned refuge to the next -
Some out there, doggedly doing the work that must be done -
Some accepting the summer's rhythm and quietly drinking
her praises ice-cold in a patch of shade.

Great Spirit, help us to treasure each circling season and these,
your ancient lands.

AT STRATA FLORIDA ABBEY
Ceredigion, Cymru, 23rd August 2000

Quiet in August sunshine
this vale of flowers speaks to me
of ancient piety and present beauty,
of peace outside of time.

Within its soil
rest abbots, bards and princes,
would-be saints, forgiven sinners,
united in tranquility.

Divinity is tangible here today in Ystrad Fflur,
where blue harebells nod under green oaks;
where White Monks prayed
and red kites soar.

EGY AZ ISTEN: AT THE CASTLE OF DEVA

Transylvania, 17th May 1999

Francis David or David Ferenc (1510-79), was a theologian and advocate of religious liberty. He founded the Transylvanian / Hungarian Unitarian Church. Imprisoned for his faith, he died a martyr's death in Deva.

God is One, he said,
and all may speak their truth in freedom.
He died here,
in this fortress on its high, steep hill.
Today it is a ruin,
for children a picturesque playground;
for us, who reverence his memory,
a place of pilgrimage.

Beneath the bright sky and the warming sun
we remember Francis David, who died in a
dungeon dark and cold - because he said
that God is One and all may speak their truth
in freedom.

AT LAKE BALATON, HUNGARY

For the meetings of the International Council of Unitarians and Universalists, 4th - 10th May 1999

MORNING - A CHALICE-LIGHTING

Another day has come to us and to Hungary's lakes and plains.
We light this chalice to greet the morning and to greet each other
We light it to proclaim hope and to remind us of those on this
continent who despair.

EVENING - A PRAYER

Infinite Spirit of Life,
Isten, God - who walks with us in the garden in the cool of the day,
who breathes through the trees,
who sings in the song of the birds,
who speaks to us as we speak to each other,
we give thanks that we are together here this evening.

We give thanks for this day which we have shared.
We give thanks that our written words of principle and purpose
have come to life in this community we have created,
this island of peace in a suffering and strife-torn world.

May the wholeness we feel in this sacred moment
be a part of the earth's healing.

Town and City

AROUND THIS FLAME
Chalice-lighting for the Ipswich inter-faith Civic Celebration of Community, 26th March 2000

Around this flame we gather,
people of this town; glad to be
together at our celebration.

To it we bring the insights and
treasures of our living traditions,
witnessing in humility and listening
with hearts open to each other.

Around this flame, rich with the
meanings that each faith brings to it,
we gather to say that in our diversity
we are one community.

THE BRIDGE

For the Ipswich inter-faith Civic Celebration of Community, 15th March 1998

The quotations at the beginning are, respectively, from a seventh-century Indian inscription, and the Gospel of Thomas.

Jesus said, "This world is a bridge. Pass over it, but do not build a house on it."
Jesus said, "Become passers-by."

We are passers-by. On our journey we cross the bridge; and though we may linger, we cannot stay.

The bridge carries many passengers. We are not alone with those of our own faith or race or nation. It is an ever-changing cavalcade that crosses over.

Each of us is engaged on our own journey. No two are quite the same. Yet the bridge has but one beginning and one end, and these we share.

The bridge is graceful, bathed in the light of sun and moon and stars. From its wide span we see a rich landscape. There is no need to rush - and miss the beauty of the moment.

The bridge is not ours. Others will follow. We must leave it clean, uncluttered and strong for them.

The bridge is wide enough for us all. We must travel as fellow pilgrims - sharing our tales, helping each other, admiring the view.

We are passers-by. We cannot live on this bridge forever. Even if we try to build houses here, we must still move on and leave them.

Let us accept the journey in faith and hope; travel together in peace and joy; and know that - for all our differences - we are but one company.

PASSING BY

Outside Euston Station, London, September 1997

I passed a beggar in the street.
I didn't pause.
I walked straight on with gaze averted.

But I had seen her sitting there - pale,
dejected, helpless; heard her mumbled
request.

I rationalized: she wants the money for
drink or drugs; she gets social security;
she doesn't really need my fifty pence.

I heard another voice - 'Whatever you did
for the least of these...'
But I still passed by - again.

THE CRYSTAL RIVER (Revelation 22: 1 - 2)

Invocation for a London District service, January 1998

Along - and beneath - the city's streets
we have come to meet and to worship together.

We seek fellowship, communion, inspiration
and, perhaps, a vision: to see the crystal river
of the water of life flowing through the city,
and on either side the trees whose leaves
are for the healing of the nations.

FAITH FROM THE CITY: FOR LONDON
January 1998

Creator, comforter, life of our life,
whom we reverence in the stars and in our inmost selves,
we pause to feel your presence with us here.

We are called to witness in this great city.

Help us to sense your divine life in the deep wells
of its history and heritage;
in the beauty and the squalor;
in the bustle and the rare stillness;
in the variety of its peoples, creeds and cultures.

Help us to draw faith from the city,
to be a blessing to its life;
to create in its midst communities
of your free and loving Spirit.

In the awareness of our oneness
and our common faith, let us join
in the communion of silence...

Ours is a bond of union too deep for words.
Ours is a union of the human spirit, rooted in the Divine
Unity.
Spirit of that Unity, with us here, now,
may we know your presence and be blessed.

SATURDAY NIGHT IN THE WEST END
30th October 1999

From The Strand the party rolls
through Covent Garden, Leicester Square to Piccadilly...
pounding clubs, pulsating pubs, electric pleasure domes;
streets surging with the beauty and the joy of youth -
lissom, raucous, many-tongued, mirthful.

A spectral presence too -
the pushers' whispered offers in the crowd,
tube-station beggars, doorway derelicts;
lost souls, wraith-like, so old before their time.

What am I doing here?
A spectator where once I was a player.

A DREAM OF INDIA
Shri Swaminarayan Mandir (Hindu Temple),
Neasden, London, 2nd September 2000

Can it be true?
In dreariest Neasden?
In sprawling dull suburbia?
Beside the North Circular's creeping dereliction?

A dream of India,
gleaming white, with pennants bravely flying,
sacred mountains rising improbably to Indra's sky.
Shiva dances here, Krishna plays and Lakshmi helps the poor.
Ganesha offers learning and good luck
to those who come to pray.

More deities are here than I can count
but they are One in Brahman, who made all.
And one are all who shed their shoes to enter:
sadhus, seekers, disciples of the guru;
those who come to worship and to wonder.

Within the hum of London
hear the Om of eternity.

AN OASIS FOR THE SPIRIT

For the dedication of the new Cross Street Chapel, Manchester
6th March 1998

God of this city,
whose face is the faces of its people in all their variety,
whose voice we hear in their words of love,
their cries of pain, their calls for justice,
be with us here tonight.

We have gathered to dedicate this house to your worship and service;
Make us, we ask, the channels of your blessing upon it.
Through us, may it become a place of praise and thanksgiving,
the home of living, loving community.
Through us, may it become a centre for the celebration of life's joys and blessings.
Through us, may it become a place of prophecy and a refuge for the weary - an oasis for the human spirit amidst the city's turmoil.

We are conscious of the heritage to which we are heirs.
We give thanks for the generations who have witnessed to your love and truth on this piece of ground; made it holy with their devotions.
But help us to be free of history's sweet burden,
to be your witnesses in the here and now,
to make this a place of living faith in this present moment.

And grant us a vision to lead us on.
A vision of this city as a place where none shall dwell in poverty and despair, in bondage or in fear.
A place where people of faith, people of goodwill, shall be true to the one divine heart of their diverse traditions and so join hands to build peace and plenty wherever there is discord, misery and want.

God of this city,
bless this house of hope.
May the flame of your Spirit burn bright in
the chalice of communion that we have kindled here anew.

This we ask in the name of all your messengers. Amen.

Gathering to Worship: Invocations and Chalice-lightings

Chalice-lighting is a distinctively Unitarian / Universalist way of commencing worship. It derives from the 'flaming chalice', the now generally recognised symbol of this liberal religious tradition. The chalice of communion symbolises the community. The flame stands for the Spirit of Love, Truth and Liberty with which the community hopes to be filled, and for the martyrdom of those who have died in witnessing to it.

OMNIPRESENT
Based on words used by the Rev. John Fairfax
at the opening of the Ipswich Unitarian Meeting House,
26th April 1700

Divinity is present everywhere.
Heaven and earth are filled with God.
But in some places at certain times
we feel a specialty of presence.
May this be such a place and such a time.

TO BEGIN
Based on a report of the meetings of the National Conference of Unitarian Churches held in Saratoga, New York, September 1894.

Let us clasp hands in gratitude for each other.
May all disputes disappear in faith and all wrangling in love.
May all our individual vanities be hushed in the one great
holy spirit of God's peace.

INCARNATIONS

With thanks to James Martineau (1805-1900)

In humility
but not in shame
we bow before you,
One whom we cannot name,
lest names divide.

In humility,
because we wonder at your transcendent immensity,
at your loving ideal immanent in ourselves.
But not in shame,
for it is no disgrace to be human,
whatever the follies and failings of each of us.

You have bent into our humanity
to dwell here.
Not just into one of us - once upon a time -
but always, eternally, into all of us.

May we live with the knowledge
of who we are
- frail, imperfect, transient;
- eternal power
incarnate for a moment
in us.

Let us use that moment well.
Amen.

THE SPARK OF GOD

A chalice-lighting using words
by Norbert Fabian Capek (1870-1942)

We kindle the spark of God within ourselves
when we serve others, and bring a glow of joy
to other people's lives.

WE GATHER TO SHARE

We gather to share
our faith
in the spirit of freedom,
our doubts
in the spirit of honesty.

We gather to focus
our love in prayer,
to send it to those
who suffer and grieve -
in our own community
and in the wider world.

We gather to strengthen
the good that is in us,
that goodness may be
stronger on the earth.

We gather to worship.

A DEDICATED MINORITY

Martin Luther King once said, 'The hope of the world is still in dedicated minorities. The trailblazers in human, academic, scientific and religious freedom have always been in the minority.'

As we gather to worship today
  may it be as such a minority,
dedicated to the cause of freedom
  for all the people of the earth.

RECEIVING THE LIGHT (John 5:35)

A chalice-lighting
(with thanks to William Tyndale)

This is
a burning and a shining light,
like that which was kindled
in all true prophets.
In our worship we receive it
as we receive them,
messengers of the divine.

AS THE DARKNESS FALLS

We gather as the darkness falls
to worship beneath the starry vault of heaven.
As we join in praise let us be one in spirit with
all who pause like us to pray beneath the stars -
wherever they may be on this planet, or on any
other.

INVOCATION

Chalice-lighting for a Flower Communion

We light our chalice-candle,
invoking the divine light
that shines in stars and suns and the bright eyes of a child.

We light our chalice-candle
to invoke the warmth
that wakens the divine life in cold earth and cold hearts.

We light our chalice-candle
so we can see the divine beauty in a flower
and the human beauty in courageous love.

FIERY JOY

Chalice-lighting based on words from William Blake's 'America'

We renew the fiery joy,
for everything that lives is holy
and life delights in life;
because the soul of sweet delight
can never be defiled.

AGAINST THE DARKNESS

We kindle a light against the darkness.
We affirm hope against despair.
We invoke love against indifference.
Living Spirit
Healer, comforter
Come amongst us
Enflame our souls
As we meet in your name.

PILLAR OF FIRE
Exodus 13: 20-21

Through the darkness,
into the wilderness,
led the pillar of fire -
lighting the way to freedom.
This flame burns for freedom too.
It is ours to claim, ours to share,
ours to bring to oppression's shadow.

TO BEGIN OUR WORSHIP

We kindle this flame to begin our worship,
to signify that we, the beloved community, are
gathered once again in this house of God.
Here we celebrate our unity as members of a seamless
humankind in a seamless creation.
Here we seek peace and love and justice to dispel the
follies that divide us.

LAMPS TO THE WORLD
Matthew 5: 14, 16

Jesus told us that we are a light for all the world.
As we light our chalice, let us remember that.
May we be lamps shedding light among our fellows,
humble vessels of divine radiance to our one world.

THE ALTAR FIRE

Based on words by Ralph Waldo Emerson

Dare to love God without mediator or veil!
Be acquainted at first hand with Deity!
We rekindle the altar fire of new love, new faith, new sight.

THE FLAME OF TRUTH

Tune: 'Morning Light'

The flame of truth is kindled,
Our chalice burning bright;
Amongst us moves the Spirit
In whom we take delight.
We worship here in freedom
With conscience unconstrained,
A pilgrim people thankful
For what great souls have gained.

The flame of thought is kindled,
We celebrate the mind:
Its search for deepest meaning
That time-bound creeds can't bind.
We celebrate its oneness
With body and with soul,
With universal process,
With God who makes us whole.

The flame of love is kindled,
We open wide our hearts,
That it may burn within us,
Fuel us to do our parts.
Community needs building,
A commonwealth of earth,
We ask for strength to build it -
A new world come to birth.

Affirmation and Celebration

ROOM FOR THE DARKNESS

We are a fellowship -
a place to share insights and ideas,
a place to foster faith and sometimes find joy,
a place where we can be ourselves and let others do the same.

We are a fellowship of the liberal path,
open-minded, open-hearted - at least, that's our aim.

But is there room for the darkness,
the shadow beneath the chalice flame?
Is this a place where we can bring our pain,
our confusion, our despair?

Let us say that it is such a place,
a place for the whole of life's experience,
a place for healing and solace.

And let us not just say that it is.
Let us make it so, difficult though it may be.

WHY WE ARE HERE

We are not here to judge,
but to live as best we can,
in peace and harmony with
our neighbours, always aware
of our own shortcomings.

We are not here to condemn,
but to give such encouragement
and assistance as we can to those
we meet along the road.

We are not here to lecture others on goodness,
but to ask how well we match up
to the best that we know, the vision
in our souls, and then try harder.

We are not here to claim a place with the 'elect',
a place in heaven,
but to live on this earth with love in our hearts
and kindness in our deeds,
just like everyone else.

We are not here to speak for God,
but to heed the divine voice in ourselves
and to be the divine presence in this
glorious, complex and suffering world.

We are here to love our neighbour
as we love ourselves; to be human
to the best of our ability.

TRUE RELIGION

If a religion is true,
it sets you free to be your true self;
it nurtures loving-kindness in your heart;
it humbles you before the Ultimate - and your neighbour.

If a religion is true,
it challenges your conscience and opens your mind;
it makes you responsible for yourself and your world;
it stirs you to seek the liberty and wellbeing of others.

If a religion is true,
it deepens your awareness and nourishes your spirit;
it brings you comfort and strength in grief and trial;
it connects you to other people and to the life of the universe.

If a religion is true,
it will care less for dogma and doctrine than it will for love;
it will care less for rules and customs than it will for compassion;
it will care less for the gods we make than for the people we are.

May ours be a true religion!

OUR FELLOWSHIP: A LITANY

Soul of the cosmos, Spirit of love, be manifest in our worship to inspire and to bless.
May our worship be blessed.

May we feel between us a kinship too deep for words.
We celebrate the ties that make us one.

We celebrate this fellowship of the liberal faith; grant it strength and vision to be a blessing to the earth.
The global commonwealth begins with us.

The global commonwealth, the world made one in peace and plenty
where justice reigns with love and all are valued.
What matters is that we build a better world.

What matters is that our faith should make us better people; only so can we build a better world.

We reach out in welcome to all who share the vision and the will to make it real.

We reach out to the soul-hunger of our times, earthing its dreams and yearnings with tested insights and tempering reason, offering comfort to its casualties.

To this fellowship we pledge our support, and to the free and loving faith it upholds.

Divine Spirit, in us and among us, bless our fellowship and make of it a foretaste of the world's healing.

VICTORY

An adaptation of Norbert Capek's last prayer, Dachau, October 1942. Can be said responsively.

Dr. Norbert Capek: founder of modern Czech Unitarianism, originator of the Flower Communion, and minister to the Prague Unitarian congregation. Arrested by the Gestapo for his opposition to Nazi tyranny, he was imprisoned in the Dachau concentration camp before dying a martyr's death in Hartheim Castle, near Linz, Austria.

It is worthwhile to live courageously
 And to fight for sacred ideals.

Even though I am disappointed a thousand times
 And fall in the struggle.

Even when everything seems worthless
 Still I live amidst eternity.

Be grateful, my soul
 My life is worth living.

They who are pressed from every side but remain victorious in spirit
  Are welcomed into the heroic choir.

Those who overcome their fetters, giving wing to mind and spirit
  Are entering victory's golden age.

FOR THE DEDICATION OF A FLAMING CHALICE

Ipswich Unitarian Meeting House, 10th October 1999.
Said responsively.

We, the community of this Meeting House, receive with thanks the gift of this chalice -
  And dedicate it to our worship.

May it stand for the loving communion we share -
  All of us equal before the ultimate.

May its flame remind us of our hard-won freedoms, and those who won them -
  And burn for the hope of a happier world.

By its light may we seek the truth that saves -
  And know the truth that sets us free.
  Let it be so!

A VASE OF FLOWERS
Invocation for a Flower Communion

A vase of flowers -
our symbol of community:
one flower for each of us,
one vase for all of us.
Each of us needs to receive,
each of us needs to give -
freely, lovingly,
and so we grow.
For this we gather.

CHOCOLATE COMMUNION
For One World Week

Quetzalcoatl was the supreme deity of the Toltec and Aztec peoples of pre-Columbian Mexico. Cacao, from which chocolate is made, was his gift to them.

With pleasure and with pain we give thanks
for chocolate - xocolatl - divine gift from
the Plumed Serpent, Quetzalcoatl, to his
people, and to us.

With pleasure because it tastes so good!
With pain because it comes to us too often
at so great a price - a price we do not pay -
backbreaking toil, meagre returns, and even
slavery.

As we share this chocolate, we give thanks
to those who grew it and made it for their
living and our enjoyment. May we pledge
to eat it today and buy it tomorrow with
them in mind.

(The chocolate is broken and shared)

Creator with many names and faces,
loving Spirit of justice, speak within us,
that in the smallest pleasures we may
never forget the demands of humanity.

ONE WORLD: A LITANY OF CELEBRATION

We celebrate the essential unity of the world -
May there be an end to systems of distrust and enmity.

We celebrate the glorious diversity of the human species -
May there be an end to injustice and prejudice.

We celebrate the web of life enfolding this good earth -
May there be an end to all that destroys our global home.

We celebrate and give thanks for the resources of our planet -
May we put an end to hunger, poverty and wasteful husbandry.

We celebrate the divine Spirit, at work within us and sustaining our one world -
May the one world vision be ours.

(The communion of silence)

We celebrate our unity here together. May what is true for us now be true for more and more people everywhere -
Until the whole world knows that it is one.

FOR HUMAN RIGHTS DAY: A LITANY

We are human beings - whatever our beliefs, whatever our gender or our politics, whatever our faith or race or nation - this at least we have in common. On that basis, let us give thanks together.

For all who have striven for human freedom and human dignity through the centuries -
We give thanks
For those who named and pioneered the rights of conscience and self-determination -
We give thanks
For those who asserted the freedom of mind and intellect, who challenged ignorance and strove to bring education to everyone -
We give thanks
For those who championed universal healthcare, for those who opposed exploitation in the workplace -
We give thanks
For those who struggled, suffered and died to win us democracy, free speech, religious liberty and equality before the law -
We give thanks
For those who fought against slavery, tyranny and oppression -
We give thanks
For those who penned the testaments of liberty; for their speeches and sermons, their books and declarations setting forth the equal rights of all human beings - and for those who claimed them -
We give thanks
For the Universal Declaration of Human Rights: composed in the aftermath of war, informed by the experience of monstrous inhumanity, its words encompassing the hopes of humankind -
We give thanks

But we cannot leave it there. As we celebrate those rights, let us also accept our responsibility to enshrine them in our hearts and make them real in our lives; to respect them in our dealings with others; our responsibility to see that our country abides by them; our responsibility to establish them where now they are ignored, violated and suppressed; our responsibility to live truly as members of one human family -

As we give thanks, so we accept these responsibilities.

Praying Together

FORGIVENESS

God of Love,
you who know our weakness
so much more than we do ourselves,
fill our hearts with the will to forgive and the grace to be forgiven.
It is so hard to transcend our hurt, our anger and our pain,
and sometimes we despair.
But somewhere deep in ourselves
your loving spirit is at work -
help us, O help us, to know it and receive it.

PEACE BE...

Based on a prayer by Will Hayes

Peace be to our fellow-worshippers,
here in this house and throughout the world -
of every faith and race and nation.

Peace be to all whose hearts are broken,
whose minds are in turmoil, whose wholeness is fractured.

Peace be to all whose lands are rent by war,
to all who harbour warfare in themselves.

Peace be to all who call on you today,
Thou source of healing love and merciful justice,
whichever of your countless names they use.

May all who lift their hearts to you
be filled with strength and gladness.

With all who turn to you in spirit and in truth
we join in worship.

AT EVERY MOMENT

Loving Spirit,
you are with us at every moment of our lives.

You are with us in the womb's warm darkness;
you are with us in the rude shock of birth;
you are with us in childhood's Eden.

In the turmoil of youth, you are with us;
in the transition to adulthood and its duties;
in the search for a life-companion to share the journey.

You are with us in the fearful responsibility of parenthood,
and in the letting-go of our children as they grow;
you are with us as we take our place among the elders
of family and community.

In the coming of the twilight, you are with us,
and in the return to the Great Mystery.

You are with us at every moment;
you are with us in our worship here, now.
Help us to know it.

FOR THE LONELY

We pray today for the lonely - in solitude and in our midst:
those who feel alone and companionless;
those who want to share their lives but can't;
those who long for fellowship and human warmth, but are denied.

We pray for the perception to recognise them;
the sensitivity to respect their boundaries and their pain;
the love to include them in our lives - and ours in theirs,
if that is what they want.

And should we have deepened another's loneliness,
through unkindness, thoughtlessness or coldness of heart,
may we repent and turn again towards them with a new resolve.

This is our prayer to you.

THE LIMITS OF OUR WELCOME: A CONFESSION

We open wide our doors. We want to welcome all who wish to come but, if we are honest, it isn't always possible.

The colour of your skin is no barrier, any more than the colour of your eyes, or any other particularity of your body.

Your age, your mother-tongue or your gender do not debar you, any more than how or who you truly love.

Your wealth or poverty, your politics or credo - for none of these will we shut you out, or so we hope, resolve and strive.

So who can our circle not include ?

Those who come with malice in their hearts.
Those who violate the respectful tolerance we afford each other.
Those who would do violence with hand or tongue.

Those whose sickness of mind is beyond our competence to help.

We cannot cope with everyone.

We want to welcome everyone who comes in goodwill,
all who come with curious minds or searching souls,
all who come to worship, to find fellowship, to ask such help as we can give.

We wish our welcome was wider still,
that we really could embrace everyone
with a healing, loving embrace.

But we can't. We are sorry. Forgive us.

STRENGTH TO LOVE

Based on words by Rabindranath Tagore in 'Sadhana: the realisation of life'

O giver of thyself!
  at the vision of you as joy

let our souls flame up to you
  as the fire,
  flow on to you as the river,
  pervade your being as the
  fragrance of a flower.

Give us strength to love,
  strength fully to see and
  hear your universe,
  fully to live the life
  that you have given us,
  and to do your work therein.

FOR A TRUSTEES' OR COMMITTEE MEETING

Written for the Trustees of the Ipswich Unitarian Meeting

We meet to seek counsel together. To serve our Meeting and those who seek it out for solace and inspiration.

> May we be conscious of those we serve.

We would speak wisely and act lovingly, neither garrulous through conceit nor silent through fear.

> May we open ourselves to divine wisdom and
> be guided by her.

We represent the people of our community of faith. In and through them we hear of needs to be met and work to be done. Together we hear and proclaim the call for compassionate living and a global commonwealth.

> May we be open to the deep promptings of
> God in ourselves, in other people and in the
> mysterious splendour of the cosmos.

We meet to seek counsel together. May our meeting be blessed with creativity and with courtesy, with humour and with forbearance, with diligence and with love.

A WORLD AWAKE

Source of love,
    help us to love when it is hard to do so.

Source of courage,
    help us to endure when we are afraid.

Source of inspiration,
    breathe into us when we are dried up.

The world cries out for love to heal its hatred and indifference.
The world cries out for courage to heal its cowardice and weakness.
The world cries out for inspiration to heal its soul-hunger and its withered hopes.

Source of vision,
    show us the vision of a better world.

(The communion of silence)

Show us the vision of a better world:
    a world awake to its oneness,
    a world of colour, song and comradeship,
    a world of fairness, joy and festivals.

And give us the faith to feed the vision and to make it real.

THOSE FLEETING YEARS

There is pain in losing a child -
such pain as only those who have felt it can know.

And there is pain in keeping a child too.
The pain of those fleeting years as a child grows - so swiftly.
We no sooner get used to their latest stage than it is gone.
We are left with regrets for all those things we meant to do together but never did.
Regrets too for angry words spoken in haste - that brought tears to a child's eyes then and to ours now.
Regrets that we cannot hold on to those many special moments, and that we didn't always appreciate them at the time.

There is the pain of letting go,
of struggling to recognise that a child is a child no more.
Our love must adjust, but it isn't easy.

Source of Life, who gave us our children, be with them and with us, that we may grow together as we grow apart.

SPIRIT OF THE HEALER

For the nursing profession

Spirit of the healer,
Spirit of the compassionate touch,
we are thankful for those who give you flesh;
for those who are your hands, your voice.
We give thanks for those who care for us
when we are sick in body or in mind;
who have heard your call to nursing and answered it,
who answer it every working day and night.
To you and to them we say thank you.

Seasons and Festivals

FOR WINTER

God of the circling year,
we who thank you for spring's new life, summer's warmth and autumn's fruitfulness, come to you now in winter.

We appreciate the charm of sparkling frost and gentle snowfall, the special pleasures of the season, but we are conscious also of its misery and suffering.

Sometimes its darkness and its cold oppress us. We grieve at the hardship and the death it brings. Then we find it hard to be grateful for winter.

Show us its necessity. Give us the vision to see why it must be. Let us learn its lessons, hear how it speaks to us of life concealed and wonders yet to come.

Help us to bear its gloom. Make us ready to help those for whom its burden is too great. May its hidden promise of rebirth kindle our hope and show us the way.

We give thanks for winter: for its elusive beauties and its warm fellowship. We give thanks for what it reveals about our nature, and for its opportunities to use the love you give us.

PRESENTATION
Candlemas

Spirit of the Highest, who has led us here to this temple of our hope, we present ourselves and our lives for your blessing. Make us worthy of our calling, touch us with divinity. Make us beacons to the lost. Give us courage in rejection; faith in sorrow; hope in despair.

You accept us in spite of ourselves, help us to do the same. In your love we are founded; in you we are reborn. With gratitude we offer ourselves to you - may your blessing pass through us to redeem the world.

WILDERNESS
For Lent 1999

For one man, driven there long ago,
it was bare rock, cave and waterless wadi.
What, where, is your wilderness?

Marsh and mudflat, lonely shore;
wind whistling through dry winter reeds?

Moorlands, purple with heather in the summertime?
The forest, still and deep?

Mountains, eternal pillars of the sky -
haunt of gods and ravens?

The snowfields - perilous and pure?
Even a city lot the wild has reclaimed?

Wilderness - where you are alone with God,
and maybe with your demons...

Go now to the wilderness, if you dare.
Go there in your mind and soul.
Go there and be still...

...Come out now, out of the wilderness
to your cluttered life - but carry the
wilderness within you, learn its truth.

MEDITATION IN LENT

The tempter says,
'If you want,
you can have wealth, status and power -
don't you deserve them?
They are yours to take.'

Help me to say,
'I claim no special privilege.'
Help me to say - and to believe,
'There are more important things than these
and to them I'll be faithful.'

THIS DAY OF LOVE

Chalice-lighting for Saint Valentine's Day

Our chalice flame is bright
  on this day of love.
Bright like the springtime plumage
  of the birds.
Bright like the season which they
  herald with their song.

LOVERS

Saint Valentine's Day

God of love,
God of lovers,
we thank you for the supreme gift of your loving spirit.
We thank you for the love that you give,
the love that we both give and receive.

We thank you for the love that kindles when two souls meet,
that grows and deepens with the passing years.
We thank you for love's pain, by which our humanity is
deepened and made strong.

May we learn that it is love that makes us whole -
love in all its guises: the love of lovers, the love of families,
the love of friends. Love reaching out to strangers, to enemies,
to wasted faces on our television screens.

Great Mystery, you give love; you are love.
Make us to be your caress, your kiss,
your helping, loving touch to those you love.

WORKERS IN HOLINESS
For Mothering Sunday

God revealed in a mother's love,
we give thanks for the high calling
of so many of your daughters to bear
children and to nurture them.

We remember Mary and her joy at Jesus' birth;
her quiet wonder as he grew,
her anger at his disobedience,
her bewilderment at his waywardness,
her grief at his death.

You were with her in all these moods
as you are with all who share them.

Help us to feel your creative power in
the conception, birth and growth of children;
your love in the love of mothers
and of all who care for the young.

May we never demean these living channels
of your creative flow.
May we never reject those whom you find worthy.

Your creation is holy, and all who create with you
the wonders of the spirit and the flesh are workers
in holiness. May we be among them. Amen.

THE FOOLISHNESS OF GOD

I Corinthians 1: 25
For the First of April

God of laughter,
God of Jesus and all holy fools,
God present with us in the comic and the absurd,
in that which a dull world calls nonsense,
save us from taking ourselves too seriously;
save us from our own pomposity,
puncture our puffed-up selves.
Infiltrate our deadly seriousness,
subvert it with your trickster's joy.

Show us that your divine folly is wiser than our
blinkered wisdom; that the gift of humour is our
best defence against pretentious delusion.
Teach us that the eyes of the simple can often
see more clearly than those of the worldly-wise.

Grant us the courage to be fools with
the foolishness of God, and in divine
weakness may we find the strength to
live without fear.

CHALICE LIGHTING FOR APRIL FOOLS' DAY

This flame
reminds us
of the Spirit
that is among us.
So may our jokes be gentle
and our tricks be kind,
for the Spirit
that laughs with us
- not at us -
is the Spirit of love.

CHALICE-LIGHTING FOR PALM SUNDAY

We light our chalice with a memorial flame, for today we remember Jesus: his fateful ride into Jerusalem, the suffering and death that awaited him.

The flame burns too for all who have taken the same road. May our worship do them justice and strengthen us to follow them.

A COMMUNION SERVICE
For Maundy Thursday or Good Friday

We gather round this table to share bread and wine. We do so to remember Jesus, who often gathered with his friends for such a sharing. Who did so on the night he was betrayed, denied and tried.

In sharing this meal we feel our kinship with Jesus our brother. And with those who followed him, frail as they were, we feel our kinship too: with Judas, with Peter, with Thomas - traitor, coward, doubter.

One Friday morning, after a cold night in Jerusalem, after the cock had crowed, Jesus faced the power of Rome, the ridicule of his tormentors, the fury of the mob, the desolation of the cross.

What would we have done, had we been there?
What do we do when we are there?

(Silence)

We break this bread in memory of Jesus and his body broken on the cross. In memory of so many bodies broken by the hatred and brutality of our kind.

We share this bread to affirm our unity, members of one body with all who breathe the divine breath and walk the way of love.

We pour this wine in memory of Jesus and his blood shed on the cross. In memory of so much blood, shed by the hatred and brutality of our kind.

We share this wine to affirm our unity, sharers of one blood with all who breathe the divine breath and walk the way of love.

In our sharing we are united in sorrow, yet we are united in that loving spirit which filled Jesus. Let us join together in saying the prayer that he left us. (Here may be said the Prayer of Jesus.) Amen. Go in peace.

BENEDICTION FOR GOOD FRIDAY

Based on words from 'The Burial of the Dead'
in 'The Wasteland', by T.S. Eliot

It was a cruel month
when Jesus died in mockery of spring
and was laid in the stony tomb, his body broken -
the image of God.

But lilacs breed out of dead land,
roots stir with April rain,
spirits rise mixing memory and hope.

Son of Man,
we remember you on the cruellest day
and we await your rising
from beneath that heap of broken images
that has buried you so long.

EASTER FLAME

A chalice-lighting based on the Exultet, from the Lucernarium Easter Liturgy. Exultet is the opening word of the Paschal Proclamation, sung at the blessing of the Paschal candle on Holy Saturday' Lucernarium is the time when the lamps or candles are lighted.

This is our Easter flame,
undivided and undimmed;
a pillar of fire that glows
to the honour of God.
Let it mingle with the lights of heaven,
burning brightly to dispel the darkness.
May it shine with the light of Christ
and all who share his spirit,
shedding its peaceful radiance
on all humankind.

MAY DAY: AN INVOCATION

The Song of Songs 2: 11-12

May is here
and spring approaches her climax.
This is a celebration more ancient than we can know.
As we worship, our spirits join with those of countless
generations - 'for the winter is past, the flowers appear
on the earth, and the time of the singing of birds is come.'

FOR THE SOLSTICE AND FOR FAITH

A chalice-lighting

We light this chalice to greet the solstice:
our light mirrors the greater light from which it comes,
and this we celebrate today!

We light this chalice to affirm our faith:
the faith that, in our diversity, we are one,
and this we celebrate today!

SUMMER SOLSTICE

Long, long days that fade
imperceptibly into short nights;

The hush descending on countryside and garden
as springtime songbirds fall silent;

Ripening fields of wheat and barley,
whispering of harvest-time to come;

It is midsummer, and our thoughts turn to
holidays and re-creation.

And so we gather to celebrate the solstice,
the summertime - its warmth, its light, its mysteries, its joys.
Let us join in worship.

PEACE IN THE SUMMERTIME

God of summer,
whose gifts are sunshine
to brighten our lives, and
storms to keep them green,
we turn to you in gratitude
for this season.

Help us to relax
and make the most of its warmth and beauty;
to store away the memories of summer that
help sustain us through winters yet to come.

We are grateful
for times and places to enjoy ourselves -
parks and gardens, beaches and swimming-pools,
mountains and woodlands - whether we seek peace
and solitude or good company and noisier pursuits!

Help us to let go of our frantic busy-ness
and find peace in the summertime.

'SHE WHOM THE SAVIOUR MADE WORTHY'

Invocation for the feast day of Mary Magdalen, 22nd July.

'If the Saviour made her worthy, who are you indeed to reject her?'
- The Gospel of Mary.

In the spirit of the true disciple
we are called to worship.

In the spirit of Mary, whose love
was first to know that life had triumphed.

In the spirit of Mary, whose witness
men spurned and whose life they libelled.

In the spirit of Mary Magdalen,
'whom the Saviour made worthy'.

In the spirit of the true disciple,
we come to worship.

GREETING THE HARVEST
For Lammas

Humbly and thankfully we greet the harvest,
gift of the earth, gift of the Creator
who is the life of the creation.

Thank you for the life we share
and for the food that sustains it.

Thank you for the love that makes us
one with each other and with you.

LAMMAS COMMUNION

In sharing this broken bread
we acknowledge our dependence
on the divine bounty of the earth;
our unity with all people who, like us, receive
their daily bread in gratitude and humility.

In sharing this juice from the fruit of the vine
we acknowledge that we are part of the vine of life,
with its branches and tendrils in every
nook and cranny of this good earth,
its roots in the divine source of all that is.

HARVEST INVOCATION

The last cornfield is cut
and woodpigeons glean the stubble.
Once more the harvest is in.
Once more the cycle is complete.
Once more we gather to give thanks.

THE HARVEST IS IN

The harvest is in,
the evenings lengthen,
the summer is gone
and autumn is here -
come and give thanks
for the earth and her bounty,
come and worship the God
of the circling year.

ON THIS DAY

Meditation on the saints for September 22nd, the Martyrs of Agaunum; Phocas of Sinope; Thomas, bishop of Villanueva.

On this day,
we honour 'the Theban legion', the Christian soldiers of Agaunum, who placed loyalty to God and conscience before the unjust orders of Rome's Empire, and were prepared to take the consequences.
May we, like them,
have courage to be true to martyred faith.

On this day,
we honour Phocas the gardener, singled out to die for his faith on the Black Sea shore, yet who welcomed those who came to kill him with peace and hospitality.
May we, like him,
have the love to show our enemies a better way.

On this day,
we honour Thomas of Villanueva, whose fervent heart was turned to God in prayer and to the poor in generosity.
May we know these words of his and heed them,
"Anticipate the needs of those who are ashamed to beg,
for to make them ask for help is to make them buy it."

On this day,
we honour the legends and the truth of these Christian saints,
that we may learn to be the truer instruments of God.

OUR DANCE

Opening and closing words in memory of the Rev. Frank Clabburn (1947-2000), on whose poem, 'Falling Leaves', they are based

In this season of the fall,
when bright, falling leaves
dance around us
like children playing,
we come to walk together
the paths of peace.

*

May our dance be part of All,
and when we have danced our dance
may we fall and rest
then tread
a path of sought-for peace.

THE BEAUTY THAT IS AUTUMN

God of the earth, divine mystery,
whom we perceive in creation's majesty,
we pause in wonder before the beauty that is autumn.

We are grateful for the glory of the dying leaves,
on their way from greenness to leaf-mould -
but so much more.

We give thanks for migrating birds:
those that filled the summer woods and skies,
but have now gone;
those who seek our winter land
in flight from fiercer cold.

We are grateful too for the strange ways
of fungus and toadstool,
drawing brief lives from death and decay,
yet so soon dead and decaying themselves.

For all that enriches our lives in this season,
for all that awakens our souls to the splendour of life
- so varied, so ever-changing -
we offer our gratitude.

Make us worthy of the world that is in our care.

ALL SOULS - BLESSED ARE THEY THAT REMEMBER

In this season of remembrance
we remember - each of us -
those we loved and still love
who have died.
In the silence
let us name them in our hearts
and bring their faces to our mind's eye...

Giving thanks for our remembering,
we pray to be the channels of God's love
to those who mourn today.

FLAME OF REMEMBRANCE

Our flame is lit.
As it burns and flickers
we remember lives
that danced and flickered like tongues of fire
until snuffed out by war's cold fingers.
In our worship we remember and, perhaps, rekindle them.

St. EDMUND'S DAY

A Chalice- / Candle-lighting for 20th November

'Edmund, that martyr of renown,
None holier wore the English crown,
Carried this day the glorious palm,
Triumphant, into heavenly calm.'
- from an 11th-century hymn

We kindle our flame of faith upon Saint Edmund's Day,
remembering all who die for truth and God and those

they seek to save, with prayers for their eternal rest.
Grant us the courage to drink of the same cup, if it should pass to us.

A LITANY FOR ADVENT

It is Advent. Expectation rises. the cards arrive, the candles are lit. The children can't wait.
Let Christmas come!

The lights go up in homes, in streets, in public squares. Shopping reaches fever pitch and tempers fray.
Let Christmas come!

The ancient story is retold. Tea-towelled shepherds, wise men in dressing-gowns, follow the tinsel star to a myriad youthful Bethlehems.
Let Christmas come!

Carol-singers take to the streets for causes worthy and causes dubious, hoping perhaps for mince-pies and mulled wine as their reward.
Let Christmas come!

From fan-vaulted magnificence to vandalised resilience, every chapel and church prepares to greet Emmanuel.
Let Christmas come!

Let us pause for breath: to listen to the turning earth, to feel the childhood magic stirring in our memories,
and maybe hear the angels sing.
Let us join in the communion of silence...

It is Advent. In the darkness hope will be reborn again.
Let it come to us. Let it come through us.
Let Christmas come!

CHRISTMAS CREDO

I believe that there is light in darkness.
I believe that there is truth in myth.
I believe that there is divinity in every birth.
I believe that we must heed the angels' song.
I believe that we must welcome the Christ-child,
for he is every child, the world's future.

I believe we must admit that Herod is real,
that his soldiers are real, that the closed hearts
of Bethlehem are real - real in our world and
real in us. I believe we must remember this
at Christmas yet not lose hope.

I believe that we must seek the heart of Christmas -
its joyous love, its star-lit mystery, its peaceful
pleasures. Find these and we find its power.
I believe this power can redeem us - open the
heart's doors to divine innocence.

I believe that Herod can be defeated, that Scrooge
can be healed, that our humanity can enflesh the
loving, living God.

I believe that this is the meaning of Christmas.

A SEASON NOT A DAY

Christmas is a season, not a day -
it isn't over yet.
It began when tills fell silent Christmas Eve,
and is ours now to reclaim.

Let's make it a time for our refreshment,
a time to re-create our jaded lives,
sharing the love that Jesus came to teach.
Let's celebrate through all of Christmas,
that we may carry its light through all the coming year.
Let it be so! Go in peace!

CHRISTMAS AFTERMATH

Thou out of whose mystery came Jesus to show your love for us; who gave us Christmas as a time of hope, be with us as the world closes in once again.

We want our Christmas faith in the power of peace to be a faith for the whole year.
We want our Christmas spirit of love and goodwill to be a spirit for the whole year.

We would believe that Christmas promise is mightier than the world's betrayal - help thou our unbelief.

In the aftermath grant us the clarity of a bright winter's morning, a pure vision to follow for the world's healing. And give us the dedication to make it real.

Passage

For those entering the ministry

CHALICE-LIGHTING

We light this chalice with a pure flame -
 the flame of freedom, which we cherish,
 the flame of prophecy, to which we are called,
 the flame of inspiration, for which we pray.
We light this chalice with a pure flame -
 may it burn also in our souls.

PRAYER OF DEDICATION OR ORDINATION

Divine Spirit, Soul of the universe, God of love,
through us pour out your blessing on those here
who dedicate and consecrate their lives to your
service and to that of your people:
on..............................(names)..........................

Through outward sign and inward prompting, be to
them a sure guide. Strengthen them in their weakness,
humble them in their pride, comfort them in their sorrows.

Be within them a fount of courage, truth and inspiration,
and may their deeds and words be graced always with
love and compassion.

Touch them now and always with your purifying flame,
make them ministers to our community of faith and to
the world's need.

We ask this in the spirit of Jesus our brother and of all
your messengers.

A BLESSING FOR A BABY

Name…, we welcome you to the human family and to the earth, our common home. We welcome you with water, symbol of the purity with which you were born, and a flower, symbol of the beauty which is yours. May God bless you as we bless you, and may the divine spirit in your heart guide you, comfort you and strengthen you all the days of your life.

MARRIAGE BLESSING

May God bless you as we bless you.

May you keep gladly the vows that you have made,
living together in loving commitment and mutual respect.

May the affection that is between you reach outwards to embrace all whom your lives include.

And may you find in God both strength and joy to face all challenges.

FOR A SAME-SEX UNION

Originally published in *Celebrating the Flame* (1997)

Loving God, who delights in the love and
friendship that grows between your children,
we ask your blessing on……..and……..
as they stand before you, joined in union.

May they be firm in their commitment to
each other; strong in the face of hostility
and prejudice; sure of the friendship of those
gathered here today.

As their love grows and deepens, may it make
of their home a place of happiness and welcome,
whose warmth flows out to cheer their families
and friends.

And may a world in need of loving kindness be
the richer for their life together. Amen.

A CAKE FOR LOVE'S SAKE

For the cutting of a wedding cake

To make a cake
for love's sake
is a harvest thanksgiving.

The fruits of the earth assembled,
ingredients mixed and stirred
with care.

We are a harvest too,
ingredients of a celebration,
chosen, assembled,
mixed together here -
the fruity, the dry,
the fresh, the mature,
the sweet, the sour,
the intoxicating, the intoxicated!

And so to bake
our marriage cake
for love's sake.
Too cool and it will sink.
Too hot will make it bitter with burning.
Just right and out it comes
firm yet succulent,
a subtle blend of moods and tastes,
a sensuous feast.

No icing,
be it ever so smooth, ever so sugary,
can hide the cake's truth
once it is cut.
The proof is in the eating.

And so to cut the cake
for love's sake,
harvest of passion's fruit
and friendship's nurture.

Give thanks!

IN THE HOUR OF DEATH

(I)

And should the time of passing come, may the universe receive its child back unto itself. When the struggle ends may we leave with thanks for the life of earth and for the peace to come. We yield back freely the gifts of existence and receive with gladness the gift of death.

(II)

And now that the time of parting has come, O God, we ask you to receive your child back unto yourself. When the struggle draws to its close, may we pass from this world with thanks for the life of earth and for the peace to come. We yield back freely your transient gifts and receive with gladness the gifts that never die.

REMAINING DIVINE

For a memorial service

Thou whom we recognise in love,
whose presence we celebrate in friendship and
fellowship, affection and intimacy, be with us
when the emptiness comes...

...the emptiness of loss and separation,
perhaps for a time, perhaps beyond the
boundaries of the world.

We gather with a void in our midst,
left by the death of one we held dear.
Together and alone we seek comfort.
May we find it in each other and in you.

May we find it in loving memory,
in celebration of a good life,
in thanksgiving for what ...(name)...
gave us of her/himself.

Our memories are personal, unique to each of us.
Let each of us remember in the communion of silence...

We have lived with death a long time -
since first we awoke to our mortality and so became human. But we have never really come to terms with it, especially when it robs us of one we love. And we never will, unless we cease to love.

Strengthen us, then, to live with the pain, to live through the pain. To keep on loving and so remain divine. Let it be so.

IN GRATITUDE FOR A LIFE

God our Maker,
giver of life and death,
accept our deep gratitude
for the life of, *Name.*

Words cannot express all that we feel,
all that we'd like to say.
Help us to know that silence
is sometimes the best option.

We pause now in quietness,
together in our remembrance,
alone with our memories...

...Thank you for a life well lived,
thank you for work done, things created,
love given and received.

Thank you also for the healing of grief.

May those who bear its burden today
feel their spirits rise tomorrow
with thanksgiving.

This we ask in the spirit of Jesus our brother,
who trod the way before us.

Blessing

BLESSING

Loving Spirit,
be with us as we part.
Bless those who are here.
Bless those who are not here.
Bless those we love and those we should love.
Bless those who need our love and those whom we need to love.
Bless those we would love if we knew them
and those we may never love.
Bless all who love and help us to love when we find it hard.

WE HAVE SHARED

We have shared this hour of worship,
as we share our membership of this
living earth and her human family.

As we part, let us remember the ties
that hold us close, the divine unity in
which we exist, and the path of loving
faith that leads us from death to life.

SOUL-FRIEND

O Thou friend to the poor
and friend to our souls,
walk with us throughout our lives
and reap from them a rich harvest.

PARTING IN LOVE

To close some inter-church talks,
Dunmurry, County Antrim, 27th November 1998

Uniting God,
who transcends our differences
and holds us in your loving hands,
we thank you for the spirit of
goodwill and co-operation that you
have brought to us today.
Forgive our failures and
be with us in our struggles to
sense your will and to do it.

As we part, let it be in love,
with resolve to find a way forward
for our communities of faith,
and bless us as we go our homeward ways.

LIFE'S SWEETNESS

Grant us freedom from the fear of the future
that blights the present.

Grant us freedom from the too-desperate hoping
that denies this moment, now.

Grant us the freedom to taste life's sweetness
and to live it lovingly...

...to let go when the time comes,
and so be blessed.

BLESSING AFTER MUSIC

Divine Spirit,
whose specialty of presence
we feel in this, your house,
we give thanks for the music
we have enjoyed this evening
and for those who wrote it,
sung it and played it.

As we part
may the blessing of your love
- felt and celebrated here
through so many years -
go with us.
May it be so!
Go in peace!

HOMEWARD WAYS

Our worship draws to an end.

May what we have found here of truth and beauty, love and comfort, remain with us. And may the blessing of this time together light us through the streets and tunnels of our homeward ways. Amen.

WITH GOOD HEARTS

Based on words by J R R Tolkien

Go now with good hearts
and with the blessings of freedom;
may the sun and the stars shine on your faces
and keep hope aflame within you.

Alone with God

A DAILY PRAYER

Divine Unity,
One God of our one world,
One Source of all that is within me and around me,
from whom I cannot be separated,
I turn to you at this day's beginning.
Before your majesty I bow.
At your creation I wonder;
for today and all your gifts I give thanks.
Guide me in the paths of righteousness and
loving kindness to this day's end.

A NIGHTLY PRAYER

God of the darkness which enfolds me as I lie down to sleep,
to your peace I surrender my tumultuous mind and my weary body;
to your care I commit myself - and the universe.

BEING THERE
Job 2: 13

In the presence of such suffering
there is nothing I can say.
In the presence of such anguish,
such fear, such pain there is
nothing I can do - except to be there.
Help me, thou wellspring of compassion,
help me to be there when all words fail.

TEN COMMANDMENTS

There is but one source of this glorious
universe: this alone will I worship.

I will make no idols, either with my hands or
with my mind; nor will I bow down to what
is less than God.

I will take no-one's name in vain.

I will take time out for refreshment, reflection
and re-creation, and allow others to do the same.

I will respect both my elders and my juniors, and
take responsibility for myself and my family.

I will reverence human life absolutely,
forswearing violence and murder.

I will keep my promises.

I will respect other people's property,
forswearing theft in all its forms.

I will be honest, forswearing lying and duplicity,
either to harm another's interests or to further my own.

I will be content with what I have,
not allowing envy or jealousy to
destroy my relationship with my neighbour.

OPENER OF MY EYES

Based on a Yoruba praise-poem

The Yoruba are a West African people living in Nigeria.

May the darkness obstructing our vision
dissipate into the infinite shadows of the trees.

May thc darkness of the pitfalls behind us
creep out upon the sunlit grasslands and be lost.

All are forgiven.

May earth's children move freely now
in the land with eyes opened.

O Opener, open my eyes
that I may look freshly on the world.

O Opener, help me clear
the path of vision.

Reflections in Peaceful and Troubled Times

SACRED COSMOS

Fynn Valley, Suffolk, 31st July 2000

The cosmos is sacred,
but not because
some mythic deity
made it so.

It is sacred
because it exists
and because
it is where we live
and struggle to be human.

The cosmos is sacred
because we -
the created, the creating -
make it so
with wonder and with worship.

THE LANGUAGE OF THE EARTH

Listen to the language of the earth -
the wind in the trees, the rain on the window,
the gurgling stream, the roaring waterfall,
the lapping of the waves, rocks cracking in the frost,
the grinding of the glacier, buds popping in the spring,
singing bird, buzzing insect,
people laughing, people weeping, people talking.

This is the language of the earth - listen and be wise.

CHRIST IN US

Christ is born in us
when we open our hearts to innocence
and love.

Christ lives in us
when we walk the path of forgiveness,
reconciliation and compassion.

Christ dies in us
when we surrender to our own arrogance,
selfishness and hate.

Christ rises in us
when our souls awaken from spiritual death
to join the community of kindness, to enter
the divine kingdom in the world's midst.

WAKE UP!

I have a dream of beauty and
a nightmare of destruction -
but the earth's awakening
is what really matters.
So wake up!

CINQUAN POEM
6th October 1998

Creation
Interconnected, Dynamic
Unfolding, Awakening, Reflecting
Loves in our Love
God.

A YEAR OF LIFE

From birth to twenty - spring:
  all riotous, bursting, surging growth.

From twenty to forty - summer:
  maturing, seeding, calming ripeness.

From forty to sixty - autumn:
  slowing, reflecting, greying wisdom.

From sixty to eighty and beyond: winter:
  resting, letting go, enjoying bright days before the night.

In the darkness something stirs.
Spring will always come again -
the cycle doesn't stop with me or you.
For this year of life, give thanks!

LOOK TO THIS DAY

Harris Manchester College, Oxford,
4th January 2001

Outside darkness
fills the great window.
Inside, prayer and music.
As worship moves
the window lightens with the dawn
and figures form from shadows -
clearer, clearer, colours, faces -
Christ and the Evangelists,
the Mother and the Magdalen,
step forward into
this day.

PRAYER TO THE BLIND WATCHMAKER

With thanks and apologies to Richard Dawkins
Richard Dawkins, *The Blind Watchmaker*, 1986

God, blind watchmaker,
it seems we've misunderstood you all
these years!

You exploded into being long ago;
groped through aeons unimaginable,
creating - step by wondrous step - you knew
not what.

You were unseeing, unhearing, unknowing,
uncaring, unloving.

But we can see! We can hear and know and
care. We can even love.

And you made us - slowly, intricately,
cumulatively. You had us in you, brought us
to birth. We are you, come to life.

You were faceless - we became your faces.
You were mindless - we became your thought.
You were without feeling - we became your feeling.
You were unconscious - we became your consciousness.
You were without conscience - we became your conscience.

Watchmaker, creator - you are blind no longer,
the light breaks for you as well as us.

Retreat

Great Hucklow, Derbyshire, July 1997

PILGRIMAGE

In company we make our pilgrimage,
to places hallowed by our journeying
and by our sharing along the road.
As paths meet and merge and separate
then meet again, may we be conscious
that through space and time we travel
in a mighty company, the cavalcade of
humankind.

QUEST

The quest is to a fabled goal that few may reach, and yet the vision leads us on - through a landscape of wonders. Let us notice these wonders, open up to their message and, maybe, by unexpected routes, we'll attain to more than we ever dreamed.

WILDERNESS

From wilderness to community, from solitude to company, we return. These are the poles of our existence. May we fear neither ourselves nor each other, and may what we learn in our aloneness deepen our sense of being at one with our neighbour, with our own true selves and so with the divine root of being which we share.

MOMENTS AND HOURS

Great Hucklow, Derbyshire, July 1997

We have shared moments and hours.
We have walked together and alone.

We have found secret ways
and wonders beneath our feet.

We have looked
and seen things for the first time.

We have heard messages for our souls
in the summer breeze.

We have had chance meetings
that opened windows into ourselves.

We have seen miracles.

We have set out on new paths
with doubt and trepidation.

We have walked in beauty.
We have remembered.

We have felt our spirits lift and take flight.

We have found serenity and peace,
communion and laughter.

We have been still.
We have solved riddles.

We have felt creation's power.
We have felt God's presence in each other.

We have felt the divine glory around us and between us.
We have told our tales and been channels of revelation.

11th SEPTEMBER 2001
For America and the World

‘Do not allow your hatred to turn you away from justice.’
- The Qur’an, sura 5.

This is no time for words, yet we must speak -
and we must speak of shock and disbelief and grief inconsolable.

How could it be?
These scenes of ruin and terror, fire and dust -
the world’s familiar things turned into hell?

This is not one tragedy, but thousands -
surging out like falling rubble to engulf the lives of thousands more
with death and fear and desperate anger.

Who could do such things? What abdication of humanity, what
profundity of hatred, what godless satanic bitterness
could so possess a human mind and drive it to such evil?
This we ask in our confusion.

And so we pray -
not sure in faith, not sure to whom we pray, or why,
but in confusion.

We pray for the injured and the dead,
not in their thousands but one by one -
  the office-worker starting her day,
  the traveller on a ’plane,
  the firefighter rushing to save lives...
we pray for their recovery or their eternal rest.

We pray that wisdom will rule the reaction, that pain will not give way to blind vengeance, that the innocent will not suffer with the guilty.

We give thanks for the human response to untold suffering: the compassion, the generosity, the gifts of life-blood. We pray that, out of evil and disaster, the divine might work some good unhoped for.

We pray that a consciousness of common humanity may touch the hearts of those who, in their own pain, might celebrate this wickedness.

We pray that those who have shown such contempt for ordinary people and their special, sacred lives may come to realise the enormity of their crime and the falsehood of the malice that perverts their souls.

And should they repent - from the very core of their being - for what they have done, grant us, O compassionate and merciful One, the grace to forgive.